A Crabtree Branches Book

CATCH the Wave

STAND-UP PADDLEBOARDING

Kerri Mazzarella

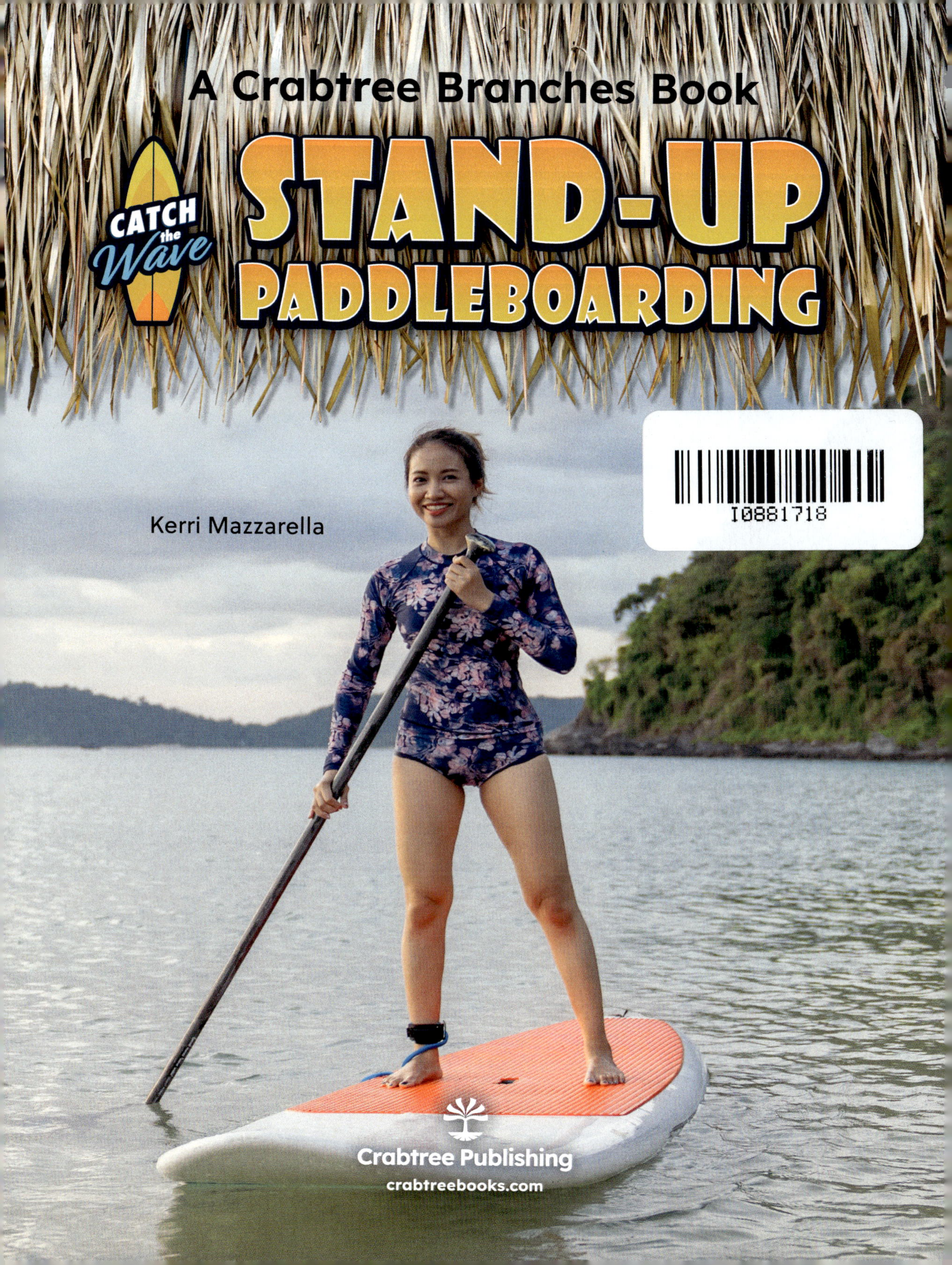

Crabtree Publishing
crabtreebooks.com

School-to-Home Support for Caregivers and Teachers

This high-interest book is designed to motivate striving students with engaging topics while building fluency, vocabulary, and an interest in reading. Here are a few questions and activities to help the reader build upon his or her comprehension skills.

Before Reading:

- *What do I think this book is about?*
- *What do I know about this topic?*
- *What do I want to learn about this topic?*
- *Why am I reading this book?*

During Reading:

- *I wonder why...*
- *I'm curious to know...*
- *How is this like something I already know?*
- *What have I learned so far?*

After Reading:

- *What was the author trying to teach me?*
- *What are some details?*
- *How did the photographs and captions help me understand more?*
- *Read the book again and look for the vocabulary words.*
- *What questions do I still have?*

Extension Activities:

- *What was your favorite part of the book? Write a paragraph on it.*
- *Draw a picture of your favorite thing you learned from the book.*

Table of Contents

WHAT IS STAND-UP PADDLEBOARDING?

Stand-up paddleboarding, or SUP, is a fast-growing watersport. The rider stands on a long board and uses a **paddle** to push the board over the water.

Fact

Some other types of stand-up paddleboarding include SUP fishing, SUP racing, and even SUP yoga.

There are several types of stand-up paddleboarding, including SUP surfing. A SUP surfer uses a stand-up paddleboard to catch and ride waves. A person should be skilled in stand-up paddleboarding before trying SUP surfing.

SUP is a fun way to explore waterways, get exercise, and relieve stress. Lakes and rivers are great places for beginners to practice their **balance** and control of the paddleboard.

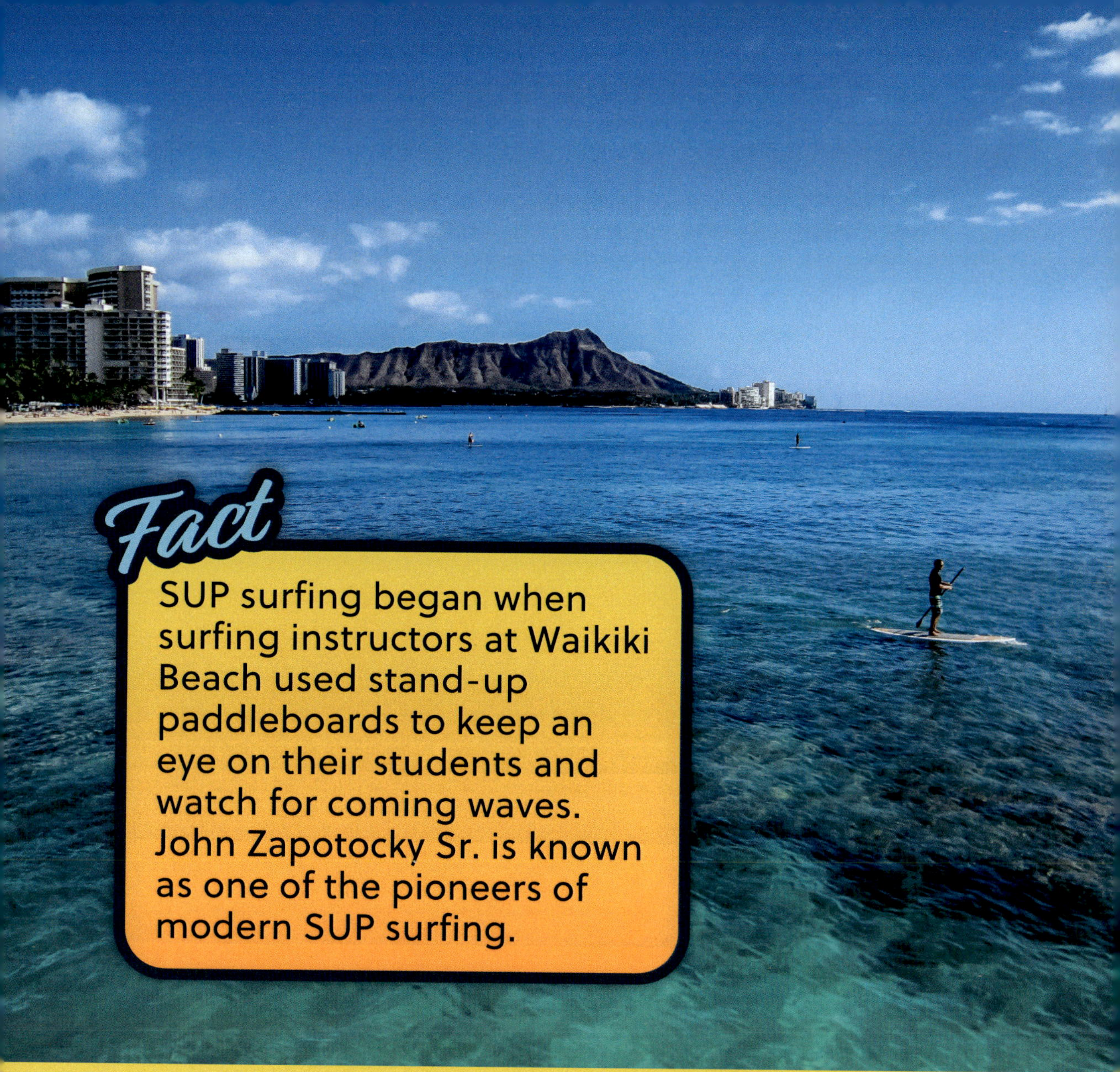

Fact

SUP surfing began when surfing instructors at Waikiki Beach used stand-up paddleboards to keep an eye on their students and watch for coming waves. John Zapotocky Sr. is known as one of the pioneers of modern SUP surfing.

Surfing is one of the oldest sports practiced on the planet. SUP surfing gained popularity in the 1940s on Waikiki Beach in Hawaii.

WHO CAN STAND-UP PADDLEBOARD?

Anyone can learn to stand-up paddleboard! Other types of stand-up paddleboarding, however, can take extra time, practice, and skill.

SUP surfing will require you to have **core** strength and balance to catch waves. SUP surfing may be challenging to learn at first, but anyone can learn with some practice.

Fact

Some people bring their pets with them when they go stand-up paddleboarding.

Stand-up paddleboarding is a great outdoor activity. It can be a fun way to pass time or a sport that is highly competitive.

CHOOSING YOUR EQUIPMENT

Choosing your equipment for SUP is very important. Paddleboards are usually around 9 to 12 feet (2.7 to 3.6 m) long. Taller people need longer paddleboards. Some stand-up paddleboards are inflatable, or filled with air. Others are hard.

hard stand-up paddleboard
$600–2,500

Fact

The bigger the board, the more stable it is. The smaller the board, the easier it is to turn and control.

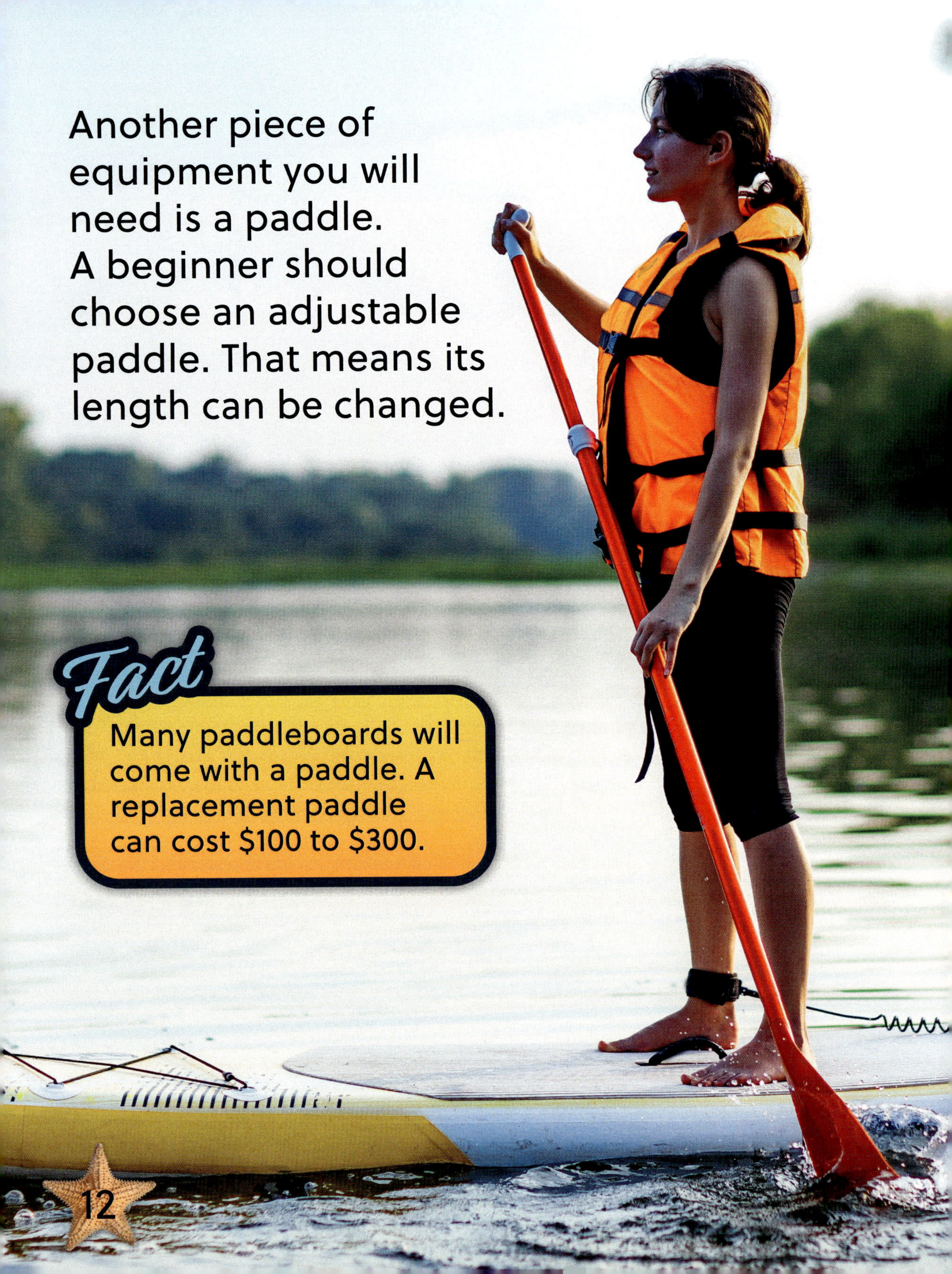

Another piece of equipment you will need is a paddle. A beginner should choose an adjustable paddle. That means its length can be changed.

Fact

Many paddleboards will come with a paddle. A replacement paddle can cost $100 to $300.

You should wear a **leash** and a life jacket while stand-up paddleboarding. A **wetsuit** should be worn if the water is cold.

leash $30–50

life jacket $50–150

wetsuit $70–200

WHERE TO STAND-UP PADDLEBOARD

Stand-up paddleboarding can be practiced in many bodies of water. Bays, rivers, lakes, and oceans are all great places for beginner or experienced stand-up paddleboarders.

Fact

Fun stand-up paddleboarding spots are found all over the world!

Fact
You could get hurt by crashing into rocks or a reef.

Beginner stand-up paddleboarders should find an uncrowded, sandy beach. It is best to stay away from rocky beaches or **reefs**.

Beginner SUP surfers should look for small waves that break gradually. A wave breaks when its highest point, or crest, falls over onto itself. With practice and confidence, you can try bigger waves.

Fact

Local surf shops can give information about which beaches are best for all types surfing.

HOW TO STAND-UP PADDLEBOARD

Learning how to surf on a paddleboard can be challenging. For a beginner, it is all about balance and **stance**.

Goofy foot is a surfing style where the surfer places their right foot forward.

Regular foot is a surfing style where the surfer places their left foot forward.

When you get to the beach, it is go time! Put on your life jacket, attach your leash to your back ankle, grab your equipment, and paddle out past the breaking waves.

Fact

You can choose to take lessons from an instructor. Lessons from an experienced SUP surfer will cost around $65 to $75 per hour.

Fact

Don't forget that practice makes perfect!

Watch the waves and choose a small, gentle one to ride. As the wave comes toward you, paddle toward shore until you start to feel the wave lift your board.

Fact

You may experience many falls as you learn. However, the thrill of catching your first wave will be unforgettable!

As you start to ride the wave, switch to your surf stance. Keep paddling, bend your knees, and focus on your balance!

FOR YOUR SAFETY

With any type of watersport, safety comes first. Never paddleboard alone. A friend or guardian should be there to help you if you need it.

Be aware of the weather, **tides**, and **currents**. These could make paddling difficult and cause a surfer to be unable to make it back to shore on their own.

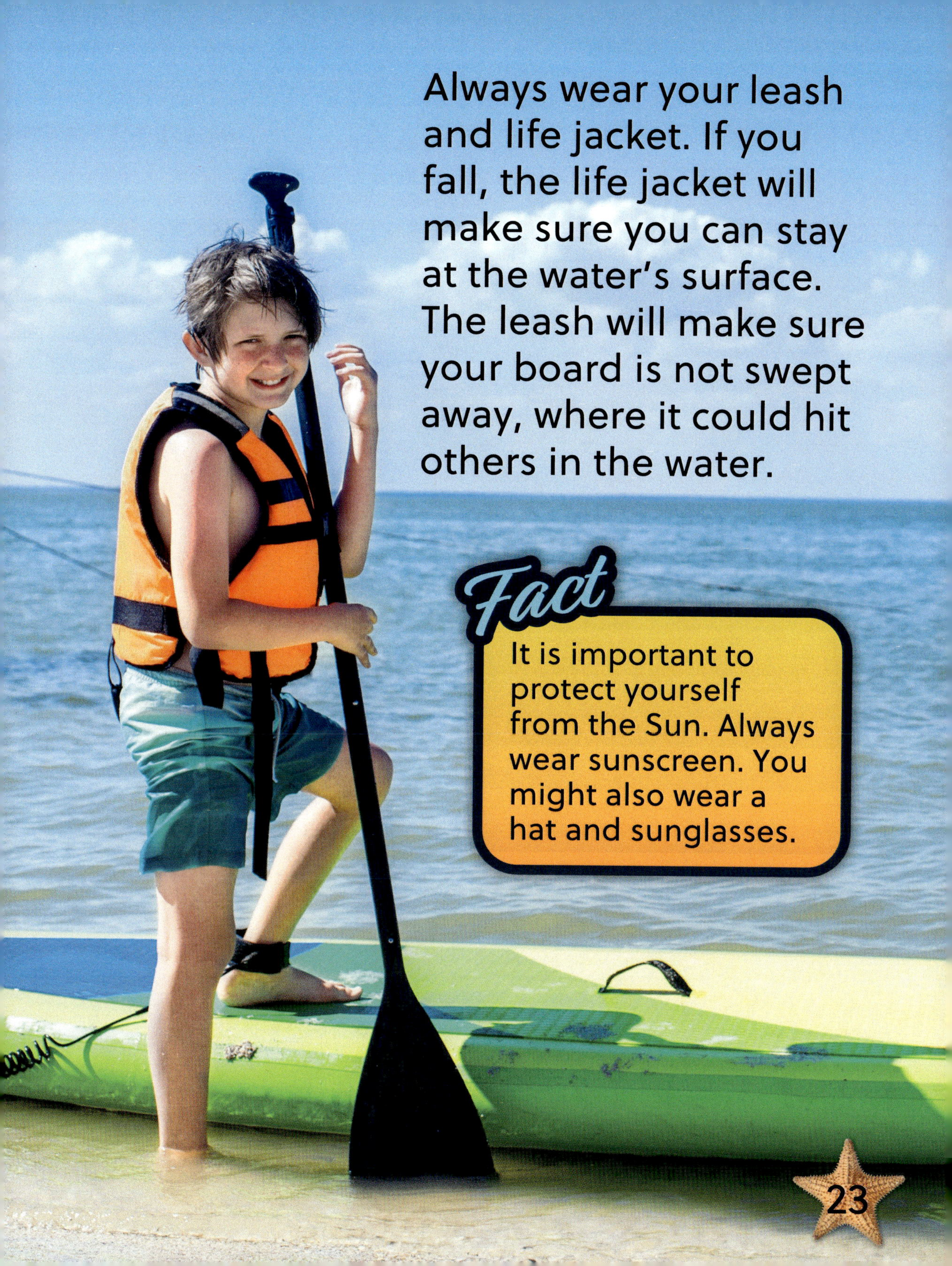

Always wear your leash and life jacket. If you fall, the life jacket will make sure you can stay at the water's surface. The leash will make sure your board is not swept away, where it could hit others in the water.

Fact

It is important to protect yourself from the Sun. Always wear sunscreen. You might also wear a hat and sunglasses.

FAMOUS SUP SURFERS

SUP surfing is a competitive sport and is **recognized** by the International Surfing Association (ISA). The ISA holds competitions for SUP surfers.

Fact

At the 2023 ISA World SUP and Paddleboard Championship, Lucia Cosoleto and Max Torres were crowned world champions.

Fact

SUP surfing is not an Olympic sport, but many surfers hope this will change in the future.

Top female SUP surfers include Emmy Merrill, from the U.S., Lucia Cosoleto, from Argentina, and Billie Scott, from New Zealand. Kai Bates, from Australia, and Benoit Carpenter, from France, are two of the top male SUP surfers.

RESPECTING OUR OCEANS

More than 70 percent of our planet is covered by oceans. Oceans help all living things on Earth.

Fact

We depend on the ocean for oxygen. It generates more than half of the oxygen we breathe!

Fact

You can participate in local beach cleanups.

You can show respect for the ocean by keeping local beaches clean. Picking up trash that is not yours is a great way to show you care.

Part of respecting the ocean is understanding the power it has. It is important to know how to stay safe in the ocean.

Stand-up paddleboarding and SUP surfing are awesome ways to experience the ocean. What are you waiting for?

Glossary

balance (bal-uhns): Your ability to remain steady and upright

core (kor): A group of muscles in the central part of the body that helps a person stay balanced and stable, or steady

currents (KUR-uhnts): Movements of water from one area to another

leash (leesh): A strap or cord that is attached to a part of the body, such as an ankle, and the surfboard

paddle (pad-uhl): A short, wide oar used to move and steer some kinds of small boats

recognized (REK-uhg-nahyzd): Officially accepted or acknowledged

reefs (reefs): Strips of rock, sand, or coral close to the surface of the ocean or another body of water

stance (stans): The way someone stands

tides (tides): Constant changes in sea level caused by the pull of the Sun and Moon on Earth

wetsuit (wet-soot): A close-fitting suit, usually made of a type of rubber called neoprene, that is worn in cold water to retain body heat

Index

Websites to Visit

https://paddlingmag.com/skills/sup-surf/

https://www.rei.com/learn/expert-advice/paddleboarding.html

https://isasurf.org/standup-paddle/

https://www.surfertoday.com/surfing/what-is-stand-up-paddleboarding-sup

About the Author

Kerri Mazzarella was raised on the East Coast of southern Florida. Living near the beach has given her the opportunity to watch all types of surfing throughout her life. All four of her children have done their fair share of bodysurfing over the years for fun! Surfing is a great way to connect with the ocean and get some exercise. Her youngest son is a competitive shortboard surfer and travels all over the world to surf!

Written by: Kerri Mazzarella
Designed by: Bobbie Houser
Series Development: James Earley
Proofreader: Janine Deschenes
Educational Consultant: Marie Lemke M.Ed.

Photographs:
t = Top, c = Center, b = Bottom, l = Left, r = Right

Shutterstock: mikumistock: cover, p. 1; Wonderful Nature: p. 4; victoria karlova: p. 5; Sanchik: p. 6; okimo: p. 7; CroMary: p. 8; Rudy Mareel: p. 9; AssiaPix: p. 10; New Africa: p. 11 t; stefan11: p. 11 b; yurakrasil: p. 12; dreii: p. 13 tl; vitalikaladdin: p. 13 bl; s-ts: p. 13 r; Maridav: p. 14; GROGL: p. 15; Wonderful Nature: p. 16; Ljupco Smokovski: p. 17 l; ViDI Studio: p. 17 r; Andrey Aboltin: p. 18; homydesign: p. 19; PomInOz: p. 20; GBZero: p. 21; Felix Mizioznikov: p. 22; Jayakri: p. 23; Iryna Kalamurza: p. 24; Bits And Splits: p. 25; Andrei Armiagov: p. 26; Prostock-studio: p. 27; ChameleonsEye: p. 28-29

Crabtree Publishing

crabtreebooks.com 800-387-7650

Printed in the U.S.A./052025/CP20250422

Published in Canada
Crabtree Publishing
616 Welland Ave.
St. Catharines, Ontario
L2M 5V6

Published in the United States
Crabtree Publishing
347 Fifth Ave
Suite 1402-145
New York, NY 10016

Library and Archives Canada Cataloguing in Publication
Available at Library and Archives Canada

Library of Congress Cataloging-in-Publication Data
Available at the Library of Congress

Hardcover: 978-1-0398-8028-3
Paperback: 978-1-0398-8388-8
Ebook (pdf): 978-1-0398-8148-8
Epub: 978-1-0398-8268-3